CONTEMPORARY K^{WITHDRAWN}HENS

MAY -- 2007

Courtesy of Italian Interiors

A STYLE PORTFOLIO

MELISSA CARDONA &
NATHANIEL WOLFGANG-PRICE

Schiffer Publishing Ltd

4880 Lower Valley Road, Atglen, PA 19310 USA

Other Schiffer Books by Melissa Cardona
Old World Kitchens & Bathrooms: A Design Guide
Traditional Style Kitchens: Modern Designs Inspired by the Past
Remodeled Kitchens & Baths: Dramatic Makeovers
Custom Kitchens: 50 Designs to Satisfy Your Appetite

Other Schiffer Books on Related Subjects
Spectacular Small Kitchens: Design Ideas for Urban Spaces
Dream Kitchens: The Heart of the Home
Kitchen Design: A Visual Library
Big Book of Kitchen Design Ideas
Great Kitchen Designs: A Visual Feast of Ideas and Resources

Copyright © 2006 by Schiffer Publishing, Ltd.
Library of Congress Control Number: 2006920918

Type set in Zurich BT

ISBN: 0-7643-2399-7
Printed in China

Published by Schiffer Publishing Ltd.
4880 Lower Valley Road
Atglen, PA 19310
Phone: (610) 593-1777; Fax: (610) 593-2002
E-mail: Info@schifferbooks.com
For the largest selection of fine reference books on this and related subjects, please visit our web site at
www.schifferbooks.com
We are always looking for people to write books on new and related subjects. If you have an idea for a book please contact us at the above address.

This book may be purchased from the publisher.
Include $3.95 for shipping.
Please try your bookstore first.
You may write for a free catalog.

In Europe, Schiffer books are distributed by
Bushwood Books
6 Marksbury Ave.
Kew Gardens
Surrey TW9 4JF England
Phone: 44 (0) 20 8392-8585; Fax: 44 (0) 20 8392-9876
E-mail: info@bushwoodbooks.co.uk
Website: www.bushwoodbooks.co.uk
Free postage in the U.K., Europe; air mail at cost.

A contemporary design incorporates traditional elements. Cabinets feature contemporary metallic laminate and ribbed glass inserts, while the cherry stain gives them a more traditional look. Open cubicles and apothecary drawers along with the ribbed glass cabinets help break down clutter and make the kitchen space more efficient. *Courtesy of Wood-Mode*

This contemporary kitchen features everything a true gourmet needs. Lateral file drawers hold scores of recipes; drawer space abounds for storing pots, pans, and utensils. Steel ceiling beams, frosted glass cabinet inserts, a glass tile backsplash, concrete floors, and a Sonoma door give the kitchen a contemporary appearance. *Courtesy of Wood-Mode*

A contemporary style kitchen with soaring ceilings and large skylights is dominated by white surfaces. The upper cabinets were installed with opaque glass fronted doors to break up the continuity of the room's look. Diagonally laid flooring injects energy into the room with the help of black tiles.
Courtesy of Montana Avenue Interiors

Quartz countertops add sparkle and color to a stark white kitchen. Very modern in its design sensibilities, the room also features beautiful, dark hardwood floors. Storage is not problem in this kitchen, where cabinets stretch from floor to ceiling and end to end. *Courtesy of Silestone*

Brown hardwood floors and counters contrast with white walls for a very contemporary look. Straight lines dominate, but hardwood floors give the kitchen a more natural touch, helping tone down the white walls and cabinets, and adding warm contrast to the room. Instead of more traditional looking chairs, director's chairs sit around a modern looking glass-top table. As in many contemporary kitchens, the appliances are stainless steel. A blackboard against the far wall makes a convenient place to record reminders and a household to-do list. *Courtesy of Bates + Masi Architects*

In this kitchen the drawers were equipped with movable trays with compartments for silverware, a lazy Susan was installed in the corner, and shallow drawers for pots and pans were included next to the oven. A walk-in pantry offers plenty of space for food, dishware, and party suplies, while a warming drawer keeps meals warm during entertaining. *Courtesy of Plain & Fancy Custom Cabinetry*

This kitchen is equipped with all manner of modern conveniences – like a warming drawer, a wine refrigerator, and a prep sink. These along with the ovens, refrigerator, and hood are made from stainless steel. Visually, the appliances provide an interesting contrast with the dark countertops and cabinets. Most of the cooking is done on the island with the warming drawer, ovens, range, and refrigerators all on or around that space. *Courtesy of Canyon Creek Cabinet Company*

Top: Cream-colored walls make an excellent backdrop for stainless steel and mahogany colored cabinets. A set of cabinets are set into the wall, as opposed to mounted, giving the room a streamlined appearance. A pair of storage containers fit snugly under the kitchen counter and are equipped with rollers to make them more mobile. A concrete slab of wall was left exposed in the spirit of post-modern industrial-looking design. *Courtesy of Pedini USA*

Bottom: This sleek, European style cabinetry is free of ornament or hardware, taking a minimalist approach to contemporary design. *Courtesy of Küche+Cucina*

The mix of natural and modern, manmade materials and
surfaces creates an interesting look in this kitchen. Exhibiting
a sleek sense of design and a grounded, earthy ambience,
the space is aesthetically appealing as well as comfortable.
Courtesy of Merillat

The owners of this kitchen wanted a bigger workspace, so a six-foot extension was added on to the kitchen. Walls between the kitchen and dining area were removed to opening up the space. Cabinets with a cherry burgundy stain have a slightly Asian feel. Stainless steel appliances are set into the wall to reduce clutter and to give the kitchen a streamlined, modern look. Floating glass shelves enhance the contemporary look while serving as a visual divider between the kitchen and the dining room. *Courtesy of Interior Dimensions, Inc./Designed by Sandy Hayes, CKD, CBD, Hayes Designs*

Warm wood cabinetry and laminated rice paper glass paneled doors grace the kitchen with a contemporary look reminiscent of Japanese design. Flat paneled padauck wood doors are sleek, but the beautiful horizontal wood grain shows through to add natural texture in tandem with granite countertops and backsplashes. The effect is a multi-dimensional space that speaks of modern design and earthy comfort. The special island design features built-in fruit and vegetable racks for easy access to non-refrigerated provisions. *Courtesy of SFJones Architects*

A vertical glass mosaic stovetop backsplash stretches across the kitchen wall to frame the kitchen window and form part of the room's focal point. Two tall cabinets flank the cleanup area, which is crowned by two open display shelves – further enhancing its role as the kitchen's attention-grabbing feature. Along the kitchen's main wall of cabinets, top shelves were fitted with opaque glass door fronts to break up the expanse of dark wood and open up the wall. *Courtesy of Joseph Hittinger Designs/ Photography by www.davidduncanlivingston.com*

Bottom: Here the theme is squares. The floor is made up of square tiles of Brazilian slate, the glass tiles that make up the backsplash are square, a square frosted and clear pattern graces the glass tabletop, and the windows, wall sconces, cabinet knobs, and chairbacks all display a square pattern.

The blue-gray background of the open shelves above the cabinets tie the cabinets together and match the color scheme set forth by the backsplash tiles and the floor. *Courtesy of Sieguzi Interior Designs Inc.*

Top: A warm cherry finish on flat panel cabinetry contrasts with black Richlite countertops. The unique breakfast bar design features stainless steel rods set into concrete, allowing hot plates to be set directly on the counter and serving dishes to slide easily from the cook to dinner guests. The island features an undercounter refrigerator for easy access from the family room and while entertaining. Overall, this beautiful, inviting kitchen is extremely functional – a great place for the family, parties, and cooking.

Courtesy of Kitchen Encounters/Designed by Mark T. White/ Photography by Michael Kaskel, Kaskel Architectural Photography, Inc.

Bottom: Functionality and a Spartan appearance often denote contemporary style. Here, straight lines and the combination of matte and shiny surfaces create a modern look worthy of repetition. *Courtesy of Italian Interiors*

Sleek, contemporary style cabinetry has been combined with rustic hardwood floors. The contrast of old and new creates a dynamic relationship in this space. *Courtesy of Italian Interiors*

Metallic surfaces dominate the look of this kitchen. Stainless steel countertops and cabinets gleam under the glow of soft white lights. Gray tiles slide smooth underfoot and shelves above the bar glow blue with backlighting. The kitchen features a bar with a wine refrigerator, a small cocktail table, an eating counter for light snacks, and a long table for more formal meals. *Courtesy of Pierce Allen*

Frosted glass doors add a contemporary touch to this kitchen. The stovetop hood flanked by two frosted glass doors form the focal point of the room. The black granite backsplash further establishes the area as the attention-grabbing feature of the kitchen's design. Two granite tiles embedded in the kitchen's hardwood floor, the table's black granite top, and the black granite countertop help to achieve unity in the room. *Courtesy of Pedini USA*

Here the wall between kitchen and the adjacent dining room is maintained but for a narrow opening, which serves as part decorative and part service functions. Glass-faced cabinets are accessible to both the kitchen and the dining room so that dishes can be taken out and used in the dining room and then put back after they've been washed. Flat paneled cabinetry doors have a contemporary aesthetic, while the wood grain adds a soft warmth. *Courtesy of Canyon Creek Cabinet Company*

Bottom: The sleek, contemporary style of frameless cabinets find contrast in the texture of green granite countertops, hardwood floors, and the kitchen's tile backsplash. Oriental throw rugs add a touch of tradition to the kitchen's look.
Courtesy of Point One Architects

The sophistication and functionality of European style fuses with the beauty and serenity of Asian design. The cabinets and the appliances were influenced by European style while the shoji style sliding doors on the pantry, a Zen water fountain, and an induction wok cook top bring in the Asian influences. The minimalist touches on both styles help them blend together in a harmonious whole. *Courtesy of Troy Adams Design*

A stone fireplace separates the kitchen from an adjacent living room. A wall of windows flood the area with light, which filters into the kitchen. Stainless steel appliances and fixtures give the kitchen a contemporary feel, while the stone fireplace adds a touch of rustic charm to this modern mountain dwelling. *Courtesy of Christina Oliver Interiors. Photos © Brian Vanden Brink*

This kitchen is rich in style, colors, and textures. Rather than a minimalist approach to contemporary design, this space shows that clean lines and simple geometry can be saturated in color and textures, and still imbue the simple elegance of modern styling. A combination of earthy colored mosaic tiles cover the exterior facing wall, broken only by the stainless steel refrigerator and plant-harboring bay windows. Two-toned cabinetry and granite countertops are rich in natural texture, adding dimension to sleek, geometric shapes. *Courtesy of Joseph Hittinger Designs/Photography by www.davidduncanlivingston.com*

Dark wood cabinets complement black terrazzo countertops. Colors in the marble tiles on the backsplash match the countertops, the cabinets, the drawers, and the appliances, bringing the kitchen together while adding interest. An integrated stove helps save space in the small kitchen while the racks above the range provide a convenient place to hang utensils. The counter wraps around into the living area, forming an eating bar with a cabinet and open shelves at one end and a concrete pillar at the other. *Courtesy of Canyon Creek Cabinet Company*

A beautiful black countertop twinkles like the night sky and offers contrast in an all-white kitchen. *Courtesy of Silestone*

The soft tans of the kitchen cabinets contrast with the grays of the countertop and island tiles. A large amount of space makes this kitchen suitable for entertaining and not simply food preparation. Here visitors can move around the kitchen, partake of snacks prepared there, and interact with the chef without getting in the way. The cabinets are large enough to accommodate extra food, utensils, and dishes for entertaining. *Courtesy of Canyon Creek Cabinet Company*

Like many newer kitchens, this one opens up into the living space, making the kitchen more than just a room for cooking. A raised glass eating bar sprouts off of the island for informal meals and snacks while a more formal table occupies the space between the kitchen and the living room, uniting the two spaces. Materials like granite countertops, slate tiles on the backsplash and floor, glass surface on the eating bar, and stainless steel light fixtures hanging from the ceiling further enhance the contemporary appearance of the kitchen.
Courtesy of Lori Carroll & Associates

This high-style streamlined kitchen features frameless cabinets in birch with a light oak stain and concealed euro hinge. Open shelving lightens the space, with a sharp machine edge to keep the profile sleek. Glass block on the peninsula heightens the modern sensibilities of the room's design. Celestial blue Zodiaq quartz countertops send this design into the space age, with modular pendant lighting to give an ethereal glow to the room. *Courtesy of Keener Kitchen Manufacturing Company/Designed by Christopher Jacobs, CKD*

Top: The dark, green-tinted granite countertops and backsplash of this kitchen complement the tea green color of the walls. Hanging lamps draw attention to the kitchen's high ceiling and add contemporary flair to the space. Stainless steel appliances also help to update the look of the traditional door style and antiqued hardware. *Courtesy of Higgins Design Studio, LLC/Design by Heather Higgins/Photography by Andrea Brizzi*

Bottom: Paired with frameless drawers and stainless steel hardware, unstained beaded inset maple wood cabinetry has a contemporary feel in this kitchen. The latest stainless steel appliances, clean lines, and simple styling also help establish this modern look with a traditional twist. *Courtesy of Merillat*

A traditional style kitchen was given a contemporary twist and upgraded look with an inexpensive remodel. Preserving the original cabinets, the designer treated them to a three-step finishing process that created a deep chocolate glaze with highlights of cream. The effect was the illusion of an age-old patina. The cabinet hardware was also updated with oil rubbed bronze. This reflected the finish that would be used in other areas of the house, like the stair railings or door hardware. Against these deep cabinet bases, the once mediocre countertops now shined in a new, vibrant light. Additionally, the old linoleum was stripped from the floors, and in its place, hand-distressed, wide plank maple with a caramel stain was laid. A hideous fluorescent light box was removed from the ceiling, exposing the natural beauty of the exposed beams. Track lighting with a unique amber glass shade was installed to provide the necessary light in a modern, visually exciting way. And to further enhance the light filtration and visual texture, the windows were treated with woven natural jute fibers. Finally, the designer accessorized the room with hand-painted Saki glasses, one-of-a-kind pottery and an antique Chinese teapot bringing just the right amount of character and flair. *Courtesy of Sarah Barnard Design. Photography by Scott Van Dyke/ Beateworks*

Bay windows offer a beautiful view of the ocean in this seaside home. The kitchen itself is big enough and furnished to be a room where all the hours of the day can be spent. Sleek black countertops and contemporary style furnishings and hardware put a modern twist on traditional style cabinetry – providing a less expensive remodeling solution to those who want a more modern look for their kitchen.
Courtesy of M & E Cross, Inc. Interior Design/John Stillman Photography

Here, postmodern design is infused with a rustic twist. Exposed beams in the ceiling are modern in their construction, but traditional in material. Shaker style cabinets are traditionally in design, but have a modern aesthetic – a wonderful approach to contemporary styling. *Courtesy of Merillat*

A "J" shaped island occupies the center of this kitchen. The curve of the "J" gives the cook plenty of room to spread out and provides space for an eating bar, where guests can enjoy food fresh from the stove and interact with the chef while he cooks. Blue painted cabinetry around the exterior areas of the kitchen provides contrast to the natural wood found at the heart of the kitchen. The kitchen's style hovers between traditional and contemporary – exhibiting characteristics of both. *Courtesy of Susan Gregory Interiors. Photography by Olson Photographic, LLC*

Nothing exists independently of the past, and the future is always tinged with the effects of history. Design is no exception. Here, the kitchen of a historic Victorian row house was refurbished using sleek, contemporary style cabinetry and appliances, while the historic nature of the space was left in tact with the inclusion of the room's original fireplace. A vibrant piece of artwork hangs above the mantel, infusing the room with color and energy. *Designed by Lori Graham of Lori Graham Lindsay Hair Interiors/Photography by Kristen Palayzo, New York*

Softly spoken in tones of reddish blond maple and rich cherry wood, this highly stylized kitchen emotes rich warmth. Intermingling colors and surfaces give the space an intriguing appeal – at once contemporary and comfortable. Appliances are concealed by flush door panels that mimic the pattern on the hanging lanterns. The island hood is sleek in its stainless appeal, with trim that adds to the attention to detail exemplified by the cabinets. Long stainless steel pulls grace the cabinet doors, while the drawer fronts feature satin nickel bin pulls. *Courtesy of Keener Kitchen Manufacturing Company/ Designed by Cindy Myers, CKD*

Red cabinetry makes a bold statement in the contemporary style interior of this home. Stainless steel appliances are flush with the surface of the cabinets for a sleek appearance. Dark hardwood floors add natural texture and contrast to modern materials. *Courtesy of Miele*

The designer opened up the kitchen to the living room by installing a clear glass wall and frosted glass door in the wall that separated the two rooms. Glass was used throughout the kitchen as the backsplash material, backlit for a dynamic effect. The two rooms were further united by using the same color palette of blue, red and white. Blue painted cabinetry establishes a cool atmosphere in the kitchen, amplified by the use of dramatic lighting. *Courtesy of Jerry Jacobs Design*

Modern European style is infused with an artistic and playful touch in this kitchen. Establishing a contrasting dynamic, the designer chose to combine sleek and contemporary elements with warm and inviting sensibility. Clean lined cabinetry features stainless steel hardware. Standing on stainless steel feet, the cabinets contribute to the feeling of airiness that permeates the room, heightened by the use of open stainless steel shelves along the wall flanking the stove. Black Corian countertops, brown natural travertine stone, and a black slate backsplash serve to ground the space, while a red accent wall adds warmth. *Courtesy of m.a.p. interiors inc./ Photography by www.thompsonphotography.com*

This large, open-space plan allowed the incorporation of three separate work areas, plus a large table and breakfast bar framed by tall west-facing windows that admit lots of light. Celadon matte-lacquer cabinets complement the multi-color glass mosaic that is installed up to the 14-foot ceiling height. The ceiling detail is a half-volute, which references similar details elsewhere in the house. The low-voltage monorail lighting washes the tile wall and provides dramatic sparkle at night. The island is high-gloss cherry veneer and includes a mandarin orange French lava stone bar top. Both the cherry wood and brown-painted wall are repeated in other open areas that are part of the kitchen. *Courtesy of DSGN Interiordesign Incorporated/Kevin Lein Photography*

Old cabinets were retrofitted with opaque glass panels and stainless steel hardware for a contemporary look. A curved quartz countertop mirrors the curved ceiling above it. Past the kitchen the rest of the ceiling is exposed in a postmodern fashion. Bright reds and yellows give the room warmth and energy. *Courtesy of Silestone*

Lime green walls emphasize beautiful dark mahogany cabinets and brighten the kitchen. One red stripe along the soffit brings out the reddish hue of the wood, while adding contrast to the green of the walls. A soaring ceiling creates an open, airy backdrop for contemporary cooking, and an austere aesthetic reminiscent of Japanese interiors. *Courtesy of Canyon Creek Cabinet Company*

A multi-colored glass tile backsplash draws attention to the kitchen's cooking center that is one of several areas set up to help traffic flow efficiently in this kitchen. A working island features a blue stone countertop and two pullout recycling bins. A cleanup island features a stainless steel sink with a commercial style faucet. Next to the stove is a food prep area with a limestone sink and a butcher-block countertop. A food storage area features a refrigerator and pullout pantry. A wine and coffee bar sports a variety of luxuries, including a warming drawer, wine cooler, and an appliance garage. *Courtesy of Wood-Mode*

Colors, materials, and various luxuries give this kitchen its contemporary appearance. The warm butter yellow of the recessed wall units flanking the stove and the cool cobalt blue of the island help bring out the tone of the maple cabinets. Modern materials include brass on the hood, and sandblasted glass snack bar and chairs. A chef's accessory tree with a lazy Susan counter revolving around it, a wine refrigerator, and an entertainment center make this kitchen luxurious as well as functional. *Courtesy of Wood-Mode*

Top: One red cabinet punctuates a kitchen dominated by black, gray, and white surfaces. *Courtesy of Pedini USA*

Center: A russet accent wall infuses this kitchen with warmth and color. Precious storage space is saved in the small urban room by hanging up cooking utensils along a stainless steel pole along the wall. *Courtesy of Italian Interiors*

Bottom: A burnt orange color punctuates a single wall in this open kitchen workspace. This modern kitchen plan was designed for efficiency and sleek style. *Courtesy of Pedini USA*

Top left: A popular feature in many new kitchens is this accessory rack, which provides stylish storage for odds and ends. *Courtesy of Wood-Mode*

Bottom left: Courtesy of Plain & Fancy Custom Cabinetry

Top right: Long gone are the days of cutlery dividers that don't fit into your kitchen drawers. Many cabinetry manufac-turers offer the perfect fitting dividers as a customized option. *Courtesy of Wood-Mode*

Center right: Courtesy of Wood-Mode

Bottom right: A knife block is conveniently located in a drawer – saving precious counter space in small and large kitchens alike. *Courtesy of Wood-Mode*

Top row:

Left: Drawer storage lets the cook get to pots and pans in a flash, without sorting through teetering stacks when the pressure's on. *Courtesy of Wood-Mode*

Right: Appliance garages offer easily accessible storage but hide the clutter that can gather on countertops. *Courtesy of Wood-Mode*

Bottom row:

Left: Courtesy of Plain and Fancy Custom Cabinetry

Center left: Other examples of drawer storage, which offers easier access to the tools of the cooking trade. *Courtesy of Wood-Mode*

Center right: This clever appliance lift offers a handy solution to the pesky storage problem – providing easy access and uncluttered counter space. *Courtesy of Plain and Fancy Custom Cabinetry*

Right: Pull-up appliance cabinets can be used to store large mixers or even can openers. *Courtesy of Wood-Mode*

Top left: A pull-out cutting board makes food preparation easy and leaves the countertops uncluttered. *Courtesy of Wood-Mode*

Top right: Backsplash panels of opaque glass are mounted on rails and slide back, revealing a hidden storage space for utensils and cooking ingredients. *Courtesy of Italian Interiors*

Bottom: Under the sink, these storage shelves pull out for easy access to the trashcan and cleaning supplies. *Courtesy of Merillat*

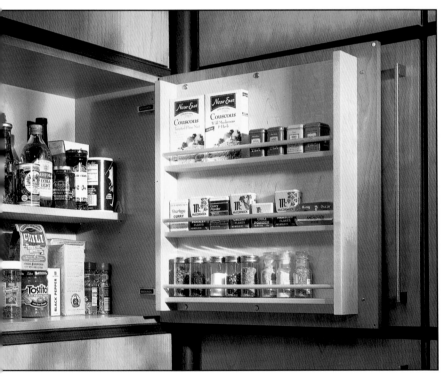

Top left: A pull-out waste basket is tucked away and out of site. *Courtesy of Wood-Mode*

Top center: This recycling receptacle makes separating trash a snap. It's easy being green. *Courtesy of Wood-Mode*

Top right: A new twist on spice rack design makes the most of space in the cabinets. Here, the desired spice is easily accessed without knocking anything else over or having to move ten other packages out of the way. *Courtesy of Wood-Mode*

Bottom left: For cooks with a less extensive spice collection this swing-out design is simply brilliant. *Courtesy of Wood-Mode*

Bottom right: A long and narrow pull-out pantry tower can be easier to organize than a standard cabinet. Here, nothing gets hidden behind taller packaging and goods are accessed from two sides. *Courtesy of Wood-Mode*

Top left: These pull-out bins are perfect for storing onions and potatoes. For less avid cooks, the bins could be used for table linens and dishcloths. *Courtesy of Wood-Mode*

Top right: The lazy Susan gets an updated design with shelves that rotate independently of one another. *Courtesy of Wood-Mode*

Bottom left: Courtesy of Plain & Fancy Custom Cabinetry

Bottom right: Apothecary cabinetry units are a charming feature and offer just the right sized fit for kitchen this-and-that's. *Courtesy of Wood-Mode*

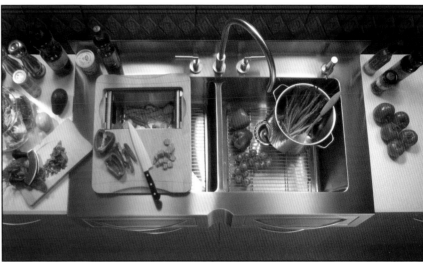

Top left: At the kitchen desk, a set of file drawers makes bill-paying and record-keeping easier than ever. *Courtesy of Wood-Mode*

Top right: Courtesy of JULIEN Inc.

Bottom left: A wide variety of stylish plumbing fixtures are available in the marketplace today. These sleek designs can help transform the look of a kitchen without a lot of cost. *Courtesy of MGS Designs*

Bottom Center: Stainless steel doesn't only have an attractive appearance to its credit. Durable and lead-free, stainless steel is a wonderful choice for plumbing fixtures. *Courtesy of MGS Designs*

Bottom right: Whether sleek and simple, or high tech like this one, the kitchen faucet should not just be a secondary consideration when planning your new room. *Courtesy of MGS Designs*

Top left & bottom left: A contemporary take on the traditional farmhouse sink, these stainless steel designs feature a convenient drawer for sponges and steel wool pads. *Courtesy of JULIEN Inc.*

Top right & bottom right: These sinks are designed to work and have been fitted with stylish backsplashes for easy access to utensils, knives, and even a sprig of herbs or a small bouquet of flowers. A built-in drawer hides cleaning accessories. *Courtesy of JULIEN Inc.*

Center & bottom left: Designed for a complete island, this sink features an eye-catching display nook behind the faucet. The nook is illuminated by fluorescent lights built into the design. *Courtesy of JULIEN Inc.*

Top left: This Aquacentre® workstation includes features for preparation and cleanup. Not your everyday sink, the Aquacentre is complete with integrated storage and cutting boards, a large sink, drain board, dishwasher, and much more, and has even been designed for the installation of custom panel doors. *Courtesy of JULIEN Inc.*

Right: As opposed to a more traditional sink, this kitchen features a circular water station equipped with bins that can be moved around the basin. This clever design allows bins to be reached from all sides of the station and moved around for multi-tasking use. A cutting board mounted on the station is also mobile, complimenting the versatile nature of the entire water station. *Courtesy of Italian Interiors*

Top: Space-age cabinets are lit for a cool blue effect – inside and out. Unlike traditional cabinet doors which are hinged on the side, these doors lift up. *Courtesy of Pedini USA*

Bottom: A futuristic cooktop design allows it to seemingly float between two grounded stretches of cabinetry. The look is sleek, adding geometry to minimalist styling. *Courtesy of Pedini USA*

The wall that separated this kitchen was taken down, now an angled island and bar serve to separate the main kitchen from the dining area and the rest of the larger room. Small details like a neon sign over the bar and fiber optics in the glass eating bar help lighten the mood of the kitchen and give it some additional character. A contemporary stainless steel post replaced the sculpture that had supported the ceiling before the remodeling. *Courtesy of Margie Little, CMKBD, CID*

Curves define the kitchen, giving it a more dynamic flow and less formal feeling than more traditional kitchens. Light fixtures hang from a curved metal bar attached to the ceiling. The cabinetry features curved corners, and even the island countertop features curvy edges and curved glass eating top.
Courtesy of Lori Carroll & Associates

The colors and textures of the kitchen mimic ones found in the desert outside the house. Rough concrete blocks resemble rocks; the cabinets are the color of sand or sun-bleached wood; and the floor is smooth and polished like the surface of a pool or a stretch of wind-worn rock. Patches of lime green dot the surface of one wall like patches of green plants scattered around the desert. The kitchen incorporates a living room and dining room, demonstrating a very sleek, contemporary aesthetic. *Courtesy of Ibarra Rosano Design Architects/Photography by Bill Timmerman*

Ground glass inserts on some of the cabinet doors, pendent lights over the peninsula, and metallic laminate on the snack bar and island platform enhance the contemporary atmosphere of the kitchen. A chef's tree also adds another contemporary element. A cinnabar finish with a graphite glaze draws attention to the grain pattern of oak cabinets. *Courtesy of Wood-Mode*

A glass topped eating bar is raised above the island for a dynamic effect. Panels on the island are a thin beaded inset pattern for a contemporary spin on a traditional design element. Glass, concrete, and the island's curvy contribute to the kitchen's modern look. *Courtesy of Canyon Creek Cabinetry*

This kitchen has a natural feel. The cabinets are finished in such a way that they look unfinished and rough. Natural flagstone was use for the flooring and the natural finish of the backsplash tiles offer an earthy texture to the room. Finished and polished pieces like the appliances, the countertops, and the furniture provide a more modern counterpoint to the overall natural feel of the room. *Courtesy of Lori Carroll & Associates*

Floating glass countertops, unique light fixtures, frosted glass paneled cabinets, and stainless steel appliances create a vibrant, contemporary style in this modern kitchen. *Courtesy of Karen Black's Kitchens and Rooms by Design*

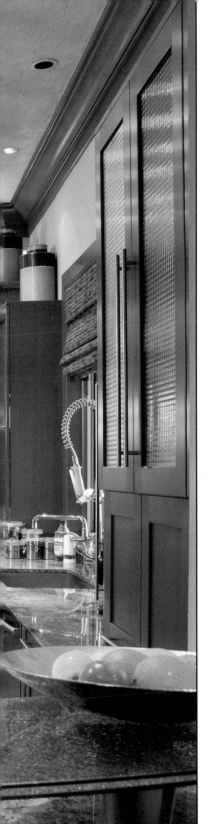

A fusion of contemporary and traditional, this kitchen takes custom design to a new level. The simple door style is reminiscent of Shaker designs, with a sharp, machined edge on the door and flat front drawer. These strict lines emphasize the long look of the frameless cabinetry. Shapes become intertwined as the wall cabinets have custom doors that simulate the kitchen's arched window. Crescent shaped glass shelves accentuate the custom curves of the glass-front doors. The geometric metallic backsplash adds a gleaming accent. The island's drum cabinet imbues the room with a futuristic look, enhanced by the wrap-around eating bar set at a lower level. *Courtesy of Keener Kitchen Manufacturing Company*

A mix of natural and industrial materials achieves unity and drives the design of this kitchen. Richly colored mahogany, light colored maple cabinetry, and bamboo wood flooring find stark contrast in stainless steel appliances and stools, and a glass island countertop. One of the most interesting features of the kitchen is a waterfall that trickles down a wall of grouted pebbles into a copper basin. Modern amenities and natural elements strike a harmonious balance in this feng shui kitchen. *Courtesy of Quality Custom Kitchens*

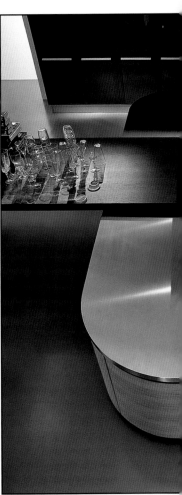

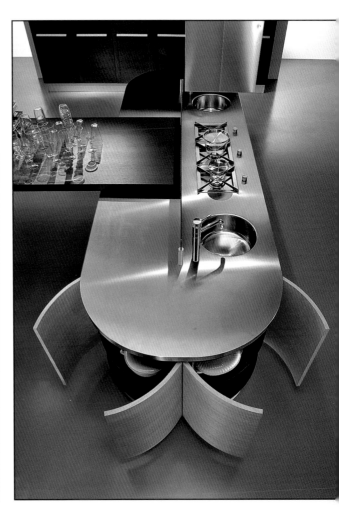

The workspace of this kitchen has been concentrated into one central area. Sharp edged geometric forms find balance in the soft, rounded edges of the island cabinetry. The island's lighter-colored cabinet doors also offer balance to the room's dominant dark colors. Elsewhere in the kitchen, the horizontal form of open shelves find contrast in the verticality of sleek pantry doors. A slick, minimalist masterpiece. *Courtesy of Pedini USA*

Simple lines and a straightforward color palette give this kitchen its contemporary appearance, while the curved island helps soften the straight edges and corners. The eating area of the kitchen was fitted with gorgeous corner cabinets. Clear glass-fronted cabinets form a centerpiece flanked by frosted glass doors. Interior lighting highlights a treasured pottery collection. *Courtesy of Plain & Fancy Custom Cabinetry*

Rows of geometric cabinets, a sculptural hood over the stove, polished stainless steel hardware, and a patchwork floor draw influence from jazzy Art Deco style. A chef's accessory system on the backsplash area above the stove and another over the sink provide space to hang various accessories necessary to each workstation. Other special features include chambered recycling center and a pullout spice rack. *Courtesy of Wood-Mode*

A wall of windows dominates this contemporary style kitchen, taking advantage of dramatic hilltop views. The kitchen's design was kept simple, with cabinetry and workspaces running along the room's main walls. The central island features a second sink for efficient cooking and cleanup. *Courtesy of KAA Design Group*

Simplicity is one of the hallmarks of contemporary style. In this kitchen, everything seems simple, yet warm and visually appealing. Instead of traditional moldings, the cabinetry was wrapped with extra-thick bronze-colored panels, contrasting in color and sheen to the sycamore doors, to accomplish a

free-standing, geometric look common to European designs. The granite-topped island was designed to be open and weightless with the cabinets raised almost a foot off the floor and a higher glass eating area, making this central area feel airy and ethereal. This feeling is enhanced with the recessed

halogen lighting system and touch dimmer electrical plug strip that leaves the backsplash free and clear of unsightly outlets. Frosted glass doors above the sink break up the large expanse of cabinetry and create a focal point enhanced by open display shelves above. In the opposite corner of the kitchen, below a light-rich window, deep drawers and ample cabinets with metal roll-out shelves and wire storage racks provide efficient storage without overcrowding the wall. *Courtesy of Kitchen Concepts & Roomscapes, Inc./Photography by John Ferrarone*

This kitchen is part of a house built in the 1920s. The kitchen was remodeled in the latter part of the 1950s and then remodeled again in 2005. The current owners wanted a more contemporary kitchen, so everything in the kitchen from cabinets to appliances were removed and replaced. A custom designed lighting system and mahogany cabinets with stainless steel handles give the kitchen a very sophisticated modern appearance. *Courtesy of Richard Gonzalez, Architect.* Photography ©Albert Vecerka/Esto

Framed in wood, the cabinet doors in this kitchen were built from a more contemporary material, stainless steel. Used often in exterior design, stainless steel is rapidly becoming popular in interior design because of its durable and decorative qualities. Here the stainless steel cabinets blend in well with the wooden frames and green quartz countertops. Like the cabinets, the kitchen's second island is also made of stainless steel. *Courtesy of Silestone*

The whole kitchen is centered on one shape, the rectangle. Drawers, cabinets, the hood, and the island are all rectangular. This creates a unity of form and style that is a hallmark of modern styling. Surrounded by shades of gray, the darker colors of the cabinets and island and the lighter edging stand out in a display of elegance and sophistication. *Courtesy of Pedini USA*

In this house, the kitchen and the living room share an open floor plan. A counter equipped with a range and a lower eating bar separates the two spaces. The eating bar is situated so it can seat four for a casual meal, or two facing the entertainment center for a quick after-school snack. The cabinets in the kitchen and the entertainment center in the living room are made from the same material, helping to pull the space together. Sleek light fixtures in stainless steel attractively accessorize the space. *Courtesy of Canyon Creek Cabinet Company*

This kitchen's stainless steel stove, hood, and stovetop backsplash find balance and compliment in the refrigerator. The curve of funky black light fixtures add a touch of playfulness to the kitchen, with its frameless white cabinetry and granite countertops. *Courtesy of Thyme & Place Design/ Interior Designer: MRJ Design Group*

Streamlined cabinetry distinguishes this contemporary kitchen with sufficient storage and counter space for cooking and entertaining. Materials include sequenced veneer natural maple cabinetry with a natural cherry wood accent, and black honed granite countertops. The stainless steel finished appliances fit in seamlessly and allow for a graceful hosting. Finishing touches include stone tile floors, tow kick illumination, and pendant lighting. *Courtesy of Corsi Cabinet Company and Bailey Avenue Kitchens/Design by Lone Albertsen*

The sleek, polished surface of a countertop finds contrast in matte finished cabinetry. Open shelves are enveloped in the wonderful, ethereal blue glow of under mounted lights. The retro light fixture and furnishings put an atomic spin on contemporary design. *Courtesy of Pedini USA*

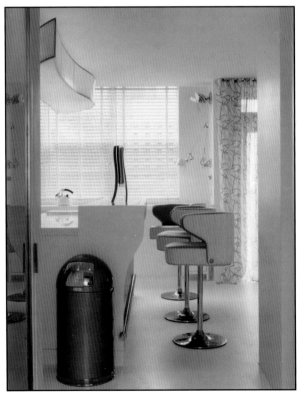

An almost all-white kitchen features gold accents on chairs, stools, and around the bar to add complement, interest, and a touch of warmth. Behind the eating bar, frosted glass cabinets provide sleek storage space. Retro-inspired chairs give the room a '50s diner flair, enhanced by metal foot rest at the kitchen island. The kitchen's workspace, which is concentrated behind the island counter, is also reminiscent of a diner's. *Courtesy of Pierce Allen*

This kitchen features an abundance of countertop space and sleek style. One of the most distinguishing features of the room is a circular stainless steel shelf placed in the corner of the central island. Black granite countertops, natural stone tiles, and wood cabinets adds natural appeal to the contemporary style of the kitchen, softening the effect of stainless steel and straight lines. Knoll chairs add classically modern appeal. *Courtesy of Lori Carroll & Associates*

Retro styling adds an atomic twist to contemporary design. A retro light fixture and Knoll island chairs are complemented by a collection of kitchen appliances designed with a vintage look. Sea foam green cabinetry fits in with the retro styling of the room, which is hip and comfortable at the same time.
Courtesy of Louis Nardolillo, CKD

Here, a contemporary kitchen has been sized to fit a small alcove. The sink, range, and all the other appliances are located in a single area for the sake of size and convenience. Like many contemporary kitchens, the kitchen is open to another room to allow free movement between the spaces and allow the people working in the kitchen to interact with those in the adjacent room. With the range facing the dining room, the cook can interact with whomever is in the dining room in an informal setting. The open nature of the kitchen helps enhance the informal, casual feeling of the kitchen. *Courtesy of Higgins Design Studio, LLC/Photography by Andrea Brizzi*

In a loft apartment, the kitchen's workspace is separated from the dining area by a set of cabinets. To match the configuration of the rest of the kitchen and provide as much storage as possible, base and upper cabinets were included with an open countertop. The open countertop also keeps the small kitchen more open and allows access to the food from the dining area. *Courtesy of James Rixner Interior Design/ Photography by Jay Rosenblatt*

A curved island evolves from a cooking surface, into a cleaning surface, and finishes as an eating surface. The cabinets behind the island blend into the wall, creating a very streamlined surface. The texture of the island contrasts with the texture of the hardwood floors and the dark color of the island offers contrast to the light walls. *Courtesy of Pedini USA*

Cherry wood cabinets, brick walls, a slate floor, and rustic ceiling beams gather influence from modern Scandinavian design. The clean lines and basic materials reflect the simplistic and functional aspects found in Scandinavian design, while stainless steel hardware, modern lighting fixtures, sinks, and appliances enhance the kitchen's contemporary style. *Courtesy of Wood-Mode*

The client of this kitchen wanted to keep the kitchen's original 1940s metal cabinets. The designer stripped away years' of paint from the cabinets to create an imperfect finish. The room's character is defined by its finishes: the metal finish of the cabinetry next to the rich natural mahogany, color variations in the poplar wood plank walls, and multi-colored olive slate floors. *Courtesy of Kathryn Scott Design Studio, Ltd.* Photography by Alec Hemer

Right: A small city kitchen is big on design. The long and narrow space is expanded by the designer's use of color and shape. The stovetop sits atop black cabinets, which serves to draw attention to that area of the kitchen, and the hood is framed by a backsplash that takes up the entire wall – thus creating the kitchen's stunning focal point. *Courtesy of Thyme & Place Design/Interior Design by Beret Design Group*

Here, a small urban kitchen allows space for food preparation with room for two people. The kitchen is still open to the rest of the house with an eating bar opening up into the next room, incorporating the workspace into the rest of the house. Rosewood cabinets contrast with dark granite countertops and backsplash, which sparkle and complement stainless steel hardware and appliances. *Courtesy of Canyon Creek Cabinet Company*

The existing kitchen was too small, so the architect modified the adjoining rooms to expand the kitchen and to maximize the amount of natural light coming into the room. The stainless steel cabinetry was aligned on either side of the room in keeping with the simple expression of design and maximizing the amount of space in the small urban kitchen. The reflective quality of stainless steel also helps to amplify light and give the impression of more space. *Courtesy of Richard Gonzalez, Architect.* Photography ©Albert Vecerka/ Esto

White, flat-panel door cabinetry dominates this small kitchen, which is completely open to the adjacent living area. The white exposed ceiling is reminiscent of cozy cottage style and provides interesting contrast to simple, sleek surfaces of the kitchen. A bright mustard wall peeks out from behind the cabinets. *Courtesy of KAA Design Group*

Light colored cabinets and white marble countertops and backsplashes give this small kitchen a clean, professional appearance. *Courtesy of Kathryn Scott Design Studio, Ltd.*

Adding height to and refurbishing the existing cabinets were the designer's primary objectives. Wood paneling was installed on the walls above the cabinets in order to draw the eyes up toward the twelve-foot ceilings. The wood paneling also provided the perfect backdrop for the client's collection of Tuscan ceramics. A table with an aluminum base, a granite top, and matching chairs with leather cushions contribute to the space's contemporary look. Cherry wood cabinets with stainless steel pulls, black granite counters, and stainless steel appliances further enhance that look. *Courtesy of Keogh Design, Inc./Photography by Daniel Muro*

Already contemporary to start with, an expansion project included additional modern features and extra storage in this kitchen. A curved stainless steel cabinet was installed on the end of the island, increasing the kitchen's storage space and available seating at the counter. On the wall furthest from the cabinet the designer created an additional wall of cabinetry which included a coffee maker, warming drawer, and a wine cooler directly into the wall – enhancing the whole design of the kitchen. Hanging lights, recessed glass shelves, and frosted glass cabinets complete the contemporary addition to this modern kitchen. *Courtesy of Keogh Design, Inc./ Photography by Daniel Muro*

This kitchen plan is the ideal layout for a small, urban apartment. All the cabinetry and appliances have been positioned around one central workspace, with just enough room for one cook. *Courtesy of Küche+Cucina*

Shelves expand upward instead of out in this modern loft kitchen. The entire room is designed with an economy of space that is often found in contemporary style interiors. Instead of cabinetry, shelves above the stove hold pots and dishes to keep all the cooking utensils close at hand. A hidden cabinet opens to reveal a refrigerator and a pantry. Instead of a table an island has space enough to sit two. The island features a small sink with an industrial style faucet and beautiful white quartz countertops. *Courtesy of Silestone*

Tucked into a separate room, this kitchen offers a simple, casual atmosphere. Stone walls and countertops are durable as well as decorative and give the kitchen a smooth, seamless look. The cabinets feature the clean straight lines and stainless steel hardware. Frosted glass cabinets and hanging light fixtures contribute to the contemporary look of the room. In keeping with the casual feel of the kitchen, a booth can sit three for informal meals. *Courtesy of RTKL Associates, Inc.*

Contributors

Bailey Avenue Kitchens
Ridgefield, Connecticut
(203) 438-4868
www.baileyavenuekitchens.com

Sarah Barnard Design
Los Angeles, California
(310) 823-7331
www.sarahbarnard.com

Bates + Masi Architects
Sag Harbor, New York
(631) 725-0229
www.batesmasi.com

Karen Black's Kitchens and Rooms by Design
Oklahoma City, Oklahoma
(405) 858-8333
www.karenblackskitchens.com

Canyon Creek Cabinet Company
Monroe, Washington
(800) 228-1830
www.canyoncreek.com

Lori Carroll & Associates
Tucson, Arizona
(520) 886-3443
www.loricarroll.com

M & E Cross, Inc. Interior Design
Palm Coast, Florida
(386) 446-8650
www.mecrossinteriordesign.com

DSGN Interiordesign Incorporated
Cedar Grove, New Jersey
(973) 857-7722

Richard Gonzalez, Architect
New York, New York
(646) 734-3743

Susan Gregory Interiors
Essex, Connecticut
(860) 767-1245
www.gregoryinteriors.com

Hayes Designs
Portland, Oregon
(503) 282-5300

Higgins Design Studio, LLC
HEather Higgins, President
New York, New York
(212) 353-2219
www.higginsdesignstudio.com

Joseph Hittinger Designs
Palo Alto, California
(650) 322-8388
www.josephhittingerdesigns.com

Ibarra Rosano Design Architects
Tucson, Arizona
(520) 795-5477
www.ibarrarosano.com

Interior Dimensions, Inc.
Olympia, Washington & Portland, Oregon
(360) 705-4342
www.interior-dimensions.net

Italian Interiors
Watertown, Massachusetts
(617) 926-2344
www.italian-interiors.com

Jerry Jacobs Design
Tiburon, California
(415) 435-0520
www.jerryjacobsdesign.com

SF Jones Architects
Marina Del Ray, California
(310) 822-3822
www.sfjones.com

JULIEN Inc.
North America
(800) 461-3377
www.julien.ca

KAA Design Group
Los Angeles, California
(310) 821-1400
www.kaadesigngroup.com

Keener Kitchen Manufacturing Company
Red Lion, Pennsylvania
(717) 244-4544
www.keenerkitchen.com

Keogh Design, Inc.
New York, New York
(212) 964-4170
www.keoghdesign.com

Kitchen Concepts & Roomscapes, Inc.
Norwell, Massachusetts
(781) 871-2400
www.roomscapesinc.com

Kitchen Encounters
Annapolis, Maryland
(410) 263-4900
www.kitchenencounters.biz

Margie Little, CMKBD, CID
Walnut Creek, California
(925) 930-6219
www.margielittle.com

Lori Graham Lindsay Hair Interiors
Washington, DC & New York, New York
(888) 336-4192
www.lglhi.com

m.a.p. interiors inc.
Los Angeles & Ocean County, California
(323) 839-8754 & (949) 278-0895
www.mapinteriors.com

MGS USA
North America
(323) 908-7618
www.mgsdesigns.com

Merillat
North America
www.merillat.com

Miele
International
(800) 843-7231
www.miele.com

Montana Avenue Interiors
Santa Monica, California
(310) 260-1960
www.montanaaveinteriors.com

Louis Nardolillo, CKD
Cabinets Plus
Riverhead, New York
(631) 727-8062
http://cabinetsplusny.com

Christina Oliver Interiors
Newton, Massachusetts
(617) 558-1262
cboliver@aol.com
Pedini USA
(800) 404-0004
www.pediniusa.com

Pierce Allen
New York, New York
(212) 627-5440
www.pierceallen.com

Plain & Fancy Custom Cabinetry
North America
(800) 447-9006
www.plainfancycabinetry.com

Point One Architects
Old Saybrook, Connecticut
(860) 395-1354
www.pointonearchitects.com

Quality Custom Cabinetry
North America
(800) 909-6006
www.qcc.com

RTKL Associates, Inc.
Miami, Florida
(786) 268-3200
www.rtkl.com

James Rixner Interior Design
New York, New York
(212) 206-7439
www.jamesrixner.com

Kathryn Scott Design Studio, Ltd.
Brooklyn Heights, New York
(718) 935-0425
www.kathrynscott.com

Sieguzi Interior Designs Inc.
Toronto, Ontario
(416) 785-1341
www.sieguzi.com

Silestone
International
(866) 268-6837
www.silestoneusa.com

Thyme & Place Design
Wyckoff, New Jersey
(201) 847- 1400
www.thymeandplacedesign.com

Troy Adams Design
West Hollywood, California
(310) 657-1400
www.troyadamsdesign.com

Wood-Mode
North America
(877) 635-7500
www.wood-mode.com